CURTIS INTERNATIONAL
PORTRAITS OF GREATNESS

•

General Editor
Enzo Orlandi

Text by
Mario Rivoire

Translator
C. J. Richards

Published by
ARNOLDO MONDADORI EDITORE
and

THE CURTIS PUBLISHING COMPANY

THE LIFE & TIMES OF WASHINGTON

CURTIS BOOKS

A division of
The Curtis Publishing Company
Philadelphia • New York

Translation ©1967 by Arnoldo Mondadori Editore. ©1965 Arnoldo Mondadori Editore.

All rights reserved. Printed and bound in Italy.

*Below: Print by Currier and Ives
of the house where George
Washington was born at Bridges
Creek in Westmoreland County, Va.
The house was completely
destroyed by fire in 1799, and the
pictures of it like this one and
the one on the opposite page,
which was done in 1930 or 1931,
were drawn according to scantily
documented specifications.*

THE EARLY YEARS

There is so little material available on George Washington's infancy and boyhood that early biographers were driven to concoct episodes of the I-Cannot-Tell-a-Lie variety. Fortunately, later biographers have spared us these soul-uplifting fables, giving us instead as distinguished a genealogy for him as is consistent with the facts and concentrating on the later periods of his life which were better documented and more interesting. The known facts about his forebears are the following: There was a family of parochial English squires named Washington living at Sulgrave, a small manor in Northamptonshire. Here, George Washington's great-grandfather John was born, probably during the reign of Charles I, to the Rev. Lawrence Washington, the rector of Purleigh. The rector had fallen foul of Cromwell's Parliament for debatable reasons: some said because he was an outspoken royalist; others claimed he was too fond of frequenting alehouses. Whatever the circumstances, his son, a seafaring man, settled in Virginia in 1657. There he did well, acquiring land and soon becoming a member of the House of Burgesses, the local colonial legislature. His son, Lawrence, made no imprint on time except that he left a son, Augustine, born in 1694, who was to become the father of George Washington. Augustine's first wife, Jane Butler, bore him four children and then died. George was born on February 11, 1732, a date which has now become February 22 through a change in the calendar.

It is strange that so little is known about his early years. By the age of 45 he had become world-famous, and many people then living must have known him as a boy, yet no one, except the Rev. Mason Locke Weems of the spurious hatchet episode, who did not know him personally, came forward with any tales of childish exploits or traits.

As there was no regular school near Augustine Washington's home, George, at the age of six or seven, received some rudimentary instruction from the sexton of a nearby church, Mr. Hobby. As Mr. Hobby's job was to bury people, not to teach them, it did not take him very long to impart to the boy all his book learning: reading, simple arithmetic and the barest rudiments of English spelling. The latter was to mystify George to the end of his life. He was never able to get the *i*'s and the *e*'s right in words like "ceiling"; blue was spelt "blew" and oil was "oyl." School children would undoubtedly draw far greater comfort from this appealing failing in their national hero than from the cherry tree-hatchet episode.

THE FAIRFAXES

The next rung on the ladder of education was a school some 30 miles distant run by a Mr. Williams. During this period George lived with his half-brother Augustine, "Austin" as he was nicknamed. Mr. Williams, who survives only dimly in history, presided over a somewhat deeper and more specialized fount of knowledge: mathematics. He found in George an apt pupil. The boy loved to count and to measure. This accomplishment was soon to become very useful.

Virginia was essentially a land of great tobacco plantations and enormous properties. During the English Civil War between the Cavaliers and the Roundheads it had remained faithful to King Charles I and to his family, and for a period it became the refuge of Englishmen who had been compromised by their resistance to Cromwell.

This world into which George Washington was born and in which he grew up was a comfortable well-ordered one. Colonial Virginia had on the one hand a well-defined aristocracy and, on the other, slaves. There was no true middle class to bridge the gap between the two extremes. Although his parents' home was a crowded and inconvenient one, it was by no means squalid, and his family, being of gentle birth, full of pride and tradition, moved easily among local society.

The young George, like his father and elder brothers before him, was to have gone to England for schooling, but his father died before the project was carried out. So young George went to live with Lawrence who had been made his guardian. Lawrence had married into the Fairfax family and settled down at Mount Vernon. The Fairfaxes were prominent Anglo-Virginia gentlemen. One of them, Lord Thomas, sixth Baron of Cameron, had left England to settle in Virginia where he had inherited 5,280,000 acres, an estate larger than the whole of New Jersey; out of this tract 21 counties have since been made. Lord Thomas, in Woodrow Wilson's words, was "a man strayed out of the world of fashion . . . a man of taste and culture" who "had written with Addison and Steele for the *Spectator*." A less admiring historian described him as an old gentleman with a hooked nose on whose breath the fumes of Madeira could be detected. But the two descriptions are not contradictory, and in any event the noble lord did take a great liking to young Washington. The young man rode splendidly and shot well; he was dependable, forthright and honest. And best of all, he said very little. Lord Fairfax decided his lands needed

surveying and for this task engaged the services of a professional surveyor to be assisted by George Washington who had been doing this sort of thing since his 13th year. This was his first opportunity for making money, and the pay was generous. He wrote in a letter, "A dubleloon is my constant gain every Day that the weather will permit my going out and sometimes Six Pistoles." A doubloon was then worth $7.20 and a pistole $3.10. The surveyors were gone a month in 1748, a happy one for George, if one is to believe his diary:

Rain'd till about two oClock and Clear'd when we were agreeably surpris'd at sight of thirty odd Indians coming from War with only one Scalp. We had some Liquor with us of which we gave them Part it elevating there Spirits put them in Humour of Dauncing of whom we had a War Daunce...

He was apparently fearless. The sight of 30 warriors with one scalp caused not a moment's worry.

Later that year Lord Fairfax secured for him the appointment of surveyor for the County of Culpepper. In this way he earned enough money to make successive purchases of land.

7

Left: the Capitol at Williamsburg. Above: view of the Yale campus. Below: a tobacco storehouse as shown in a 1784 print. Plantation owners sent their crops to an agent who sold them on the London market. The proceeds were credited to a running account. Through the agent the colonists could then buy cloth and other manufactured goods. To the right: an Indian settlement in Virginia in the early 18th century. Already there was bad blood between the colonists and the Indians. Far right: Harvard College, in Cambridge, founded in 1636. The colonists were anxious to keep their sons from growing up like savages in the wilderness. This need was especially felt in Virginia where in 1693, William and Mary was founded.

George Washington's education was not a good one, by any standards, and certainly not up to the average level of people in his own class. He knew very little Latin and no French, which in one instance proved to be disastrous (see page 12). After he had met Lord Fairfax he had free access to a good library and ought thus to have been able to supplement his sketchy formal education, but he was never a bookish man and there is little evidence that he did so. However, he compensated for this by his proficiency in accounting, drawing and trigonometry. In later years, when he had become a prosperous land owner and had accumulated a large library, most of the books in it were manuals, practical treatises and handbooks. He was the sort of man whose brain and hands worked simultaneously. His work often took him away for months at a time to distant unexplored places, where he came into contact with Indians and pioneers in a capacity which was halfway between civilian employment and military command. At the death of his half-brother in 1752, George found himself executor of his will and in charge of a vast agricultural concern for which he soon proved himself an able caretaker and wise administrator. His new responsibilities brought him into constant contact with his social equals. A typical product of the Virginia landed aristocracy, he shared their tastes and inclinations and became like them a prototype of the perfect English gentleman.

Washington shared the Virginia gentry's passion for fox hunting. The painting below, executed in 1785, is one of a series by J. L. Ferris which illustrate various episodes in the life of the general. Here he is shown at age 53 about to bestow the brush on one of his youthful admirers.

FIRST ADVENTURE

George Washington was an impressive looking man: six feet two, of dignified bearing, powerfully built with an erect carriage, sunburnt complexion, dark hair. His deep-set blue-gray eyes were spaced far apart in a long face with prominent cheekbones, a wide, high forehead, a long, straight nose, a determined chin and the largest hands Lafayette had "ever seen in a human being." He wore a size 13 shoe. Such was the outward appearance of the young man who had matured so quickly. Although he had inherited from his father 280 acres as well as some other small properties and 10 slaves, he did not take possession of this patrimony until his mother died 46 years later. Before reaching the age of 21, he had bought, solely with his earnings, 1,558 acres of land. When Lawrence's only child, Sarah, died two months after her father in 1752, he inherited her estate. And so by 1757 he was already the owner of a 4,000-acre estate.

He easily fitted into the life of the Virginia landed gentry. He was addicted to racing and hunting, and cheerfully made the social rounds of visits, receptions, and balls. He particularly liked to dance and continued to do so well into his 60's. Soon he had inherited his half-brother's rank of adjutant general in the colonial militia and had a seat in the House of Burgesses. Like his brother before him, he took a great interest in the problems of the colony. At this particular moment the major issue centered on the claims of the Ohio Company, of which his brother had been a stockholder. This company had been organized in 1747 by Governor Dinwiddie of Virginia with 19 other gentlemen as a speculative land concern. It claimed 500,000 acres in the Ohio Valley which the French regarded as their own, having explored it and indeed built a chain of forts from Lake Erie to the Ohio River and all the way down to New Orleans. In 1753 Governor Dinwiddie decided to demand the evacuation of the territory. A first messenger, dispatched to the French headquarters, had returned with the letter undelivered, foiled by the wilderness and the Indians.

Young George Washington was chosen as the next messenger. The purpose of the expedition was to sound out the intentions of the French, and possibly persuade them to take their claims elsewhere. Accordingly, he set forth on his journey in mid-November 1753 to Fort Le Boeuf, 12 miles south of Lake Erie. The French Commander Legardeur de Saint-Pierre listened to the young envoy with a courtesy equaled only by his firmness: The French had no thought of moving from land to which La Salle had laid claim 70 years earlier.

Washington's return to Williamsburg in January of 1754 was fraught with hazards. It snowed so hard that the horses had to be left behind; Washington and his companion were shot at by Indians; the raft on which they crossed the Monongahela was upset. But as always in the face of danger he remained matter-of-fact and cool.

The result of the otherwise unsuccessful expedition was to point up that sooner or later there would be war with the French.

Below: Washington's return to Great Meadows after the unsuccessful venture with the French in the Ohio Valley. The Ohio River, chief eastern tributary of the Mississippi, is formed by the confluence of the Allegheny and the Monongahela at what is today Pittsburgh. It was discovered in 1669 by the French who rechristened it "Belle Rivière," the beautiful river, a translation of the Indian word Ohio. *The importance of this line of penetration escaped neither the French, who were planning to expand southward, nor the American colonists threatened by that expansion. Hence, the struggle between them for its control.*

The French had not been inactive. They destroyed the fort erected by the Ohio Company on the site of present-day Pittsburgh and replaced it with a larger, stronger one of their own, Fort Duquesne. When Governor Dinwiddie heard of this, he dispatched Washington at the head of a ragged, unruly troop of 150 men to investigate and to make a show of force. But it was an ill-fated expedition. No one had been willing to give support, financial or moral; neither the House of Burgesses nor governors of neighboring colonies were interested. The colonial troops were unenthusiastic: ill-paid, ill-fed and ill-dressed. Washington proceeded nonetheless. It had apparently not occurred to him that he and his men might be wiped out by the superior forces of the French.

One morning, at sunrise, they ran into a detachment of 32 Frenchmen. What then happened has been reported in countless contradictory accounts. What is indisputable, however, is that the commanding French officer, Coulon de Jumonville, and nine others were shot; 21 French soldiers were taken prisoner and one fled. The French claimed that their intentions had been peaceful, that they were bearing messages; the colonists maintained that there were far too many men for a delegation. But disaster for the colonists ensued. The man who had escaped, a Canadian, quickly mustered 700 men. By this time Washington's little band had been reinforced by 200 men, but his total of 350 was no match for the French. The Virginians were cornered in Fort Necessity, a miserable, water-logged stockade carelessly built in a depression of the ground. After nine hours of surprisingly heroic fighting (given the lukewarm feelings of the colonial soldiers), they were forced to surrender. Washington signed, in July 1754, a document in which he agreed that the colonists would not build another fort on the Ohio for a year, and he admitted his guilt in the "assassination" of a French officer. A controversy which started then is still raging. It is plain that the French wanted to stamp Washington as the aggressor, but he, on the other hand, claimed self-defense. Washington also stated the French had only summed up the contents of the paper, with the interpreter conveniently passing over the offensive word "assassin." His superiors, however, absolved him of all responsibility and shortly thereafter promoted him to the rank of full colonel. To Washington fell the questionable privilege of having fired the first shot of what very soon thereafter became known as the French and Indian War.

*Below: a lithograph
by Duval and Hunter
showing Washington in
a Masonic Lodge. He was
a member but not a very active
one. Undoubtedly
the illustration was
used by the order
to capitalize on
what was only a
nominal membership.*

DEATH IN
THE WILDERNESS

To the left: Edwin W. Deming's painting of the fatal shooting of Braddock during the ill-fated expedition of 1755. It was reported that as he lay dying during the retreat, "he could not bear the sight of a red coat" but murmured praises of the "blues" (the Virginians). According to Washington the British officers "behaved with incomparable bravery"; the Virginia companies behaved like men and died like soldiers; but the English soldiers' "dastardly behavior" and cowardice "exposed" all those who were inclined to do their duty to almost certain death." Below, from top to bottom: Two contemporary etchings showing the trading between the French and the Indians. The French treatment of the Indians was far more intelligent than that of the British colonists.

Shortly after his return to Virginia, George Washington resigned his commission and went back to Mount Vernon. The slighting treatment and underpayment of colonial officers, and especially the tactless order issued by the British War Office that all colonial officers, of whatever rank, were to be subordinate to any officer, however junior, holding the king's commission—were more than a proud, sensitive man was prepared to accept.

Meantime the British government was finally stirred to action by the setback the colonists had suffered at the hands of the French. Accordingly Gen. Edward Braddock was dispatched at the head of an expeditionary force whose initial task was the capture of Fort Duquesne. Within two weeks of his arrival, Braddock had invited George Washington to join his staff. The young man wrote a friend that his "inclinations" were "strongly bent to arms" and accepted the post of aide-de-camp with the courtesy title of colonel. Braddock had a high regard for him as well as for Benjamin Franklin, of whom he wrote that he was "almost the only instance of ability and honesty I have found in these provinces." But with these two exceptions he looked upon the colonists as a discouraging lot. "Their slothful and languid disposition" rendered "them very unfit for military service." They appeared to prefer destruction to cooperation. Somewhat obtusely, he was trying to fit them for battle on a parade ground. Franklin tried to put him on his guard against the backwoods style of fighting used in the colonies, but Braddock disregarded all advice, except one unsound suggestion—that is, dividing his forces in two. When he and his men came almost within sight of Fort Duquesne, an advance British column was ordered to spread out and fire into the woods. The Englishmen obeyed, wasting volley after volley on trees. The enemy, French and Indian, swarmed through the forest and shot at the perfectly visible British troops. The survivors later declared they had not seen a single Indian; they had only heard their blood-curdling yells. Braddock fought like a madman; four horses were killed under him. He himself was shot through the lung on the fifth horse. Sixty-three officers out of 86 were killed or disabled, while out of 1,373 men only 450 escaped unharmed. Washington, who had been racked with fever during the entire engagement, kept his Virginians in hand and held back the enemy while the pitiful remains of Braddock's army raced to safety.

The defeat of Monongahela took place on July 9, 1755. The following month Washington was appointed commander in chief of all the Virginia forces. His task was to protect a thinly settled frontier nearly 400 miles in length with only 700 ill-disciplined colonial troops.

THE ENGLISH REVENGE

Despite Braddock's debacle, the English set seriously to work to recoup their losses. On November 25, 1758, George Washington was in command of the advance guard of General John Forbes's army which marched from Virginia upon Fort Duquesne, triumphantly captured it and renamed it Fort Pitt. By this time he had had enough both of the arrogance of the English and the incompetence of his compatriots. Seeing that the war was on its way to a rapid and favorable conclusion, at the end of the year he resigned his commission. His superiors beseeched him to change his mind, but he remained firm. Sixteen years were to pass before he again saw military service.

During the spring preceding the capture of Fort Duquesne, while stopping at the house of a friend on his way to Williamsburg, he made the acquaintance of a young widow. She was Martha Dandridge Custis, widow of the late Colonel Daniel Parke Custis, one of the wealthiest men in Virginia. They were soon betrothed. This cannot, despite the musing of romantic souls, have been a grand passion and love at first sight. There is evidence that George had been deeply attached to Sally Fairfax, the wife of his good friend William Fairfax of Belvoir. There are letters to substantiate the claim, in particular a sad one written to her from Fort Cumberland, in which he confessed in a roundabout way his love for her: "Misconstrue not my meaning; doubt it not, nor expose it." But Sally was his friend's wife, and he could only smother his feelings for her. And so George Washington looked elsewhere. His relationship with Martha, although not rooted in youthful romance, had a sincerity and strength which endured over 40 years.

Far left: View of Quebec in a print dated 1761. Left: Cartoon, dated 1775, showing how much concern had been aroused even in London by the colonial policy of George III. The king, with his eyes closed, is being drawn into an open chasm by two horses named Pride and Obstinacy who are trampling on the Constitution and the Magna Carta while the national credit is vanishing into the air.

Below: the death of Wolfe as painted by the well-known artist, Benjamin West, who was born in America but later settled in London where he became court painter. This famous painting, done in 1771, is in the National Gallery of Ottawa. General James Wolfe was mortally wounded on the Plains of Abraham on September 13, 1759, during the battle at which Montcalm was also killed. The French commander, despite the lack of support from France, fought brilliantly but lost the decisive battle which cost France her Canadian possessions.

MARRIAGE

The wedding of Colonel Washington and Martha Dandridge Custis, which took place on January 6, 1759, at the bride's home, was a resplendent affair. While the young couple were perhaps not giddily in love, they had for each other a contented, calm affection. Martha proved a faithful wife, an accomplished housekeeper, and a social asset. He, in turn, was a model husband. He took over the management of her estate and the guardianship of her two young children by her first marriage, Patsy and Jack Custis, whom he treated as his own. His wife's marriage portion, added to his own estates, made him one of the richest landowners in Virginia at the age of 27. It has frequently been alleged that he owed his financial success to an expedient marriage. This is unfair; the inheritance from his brother had been substantial, and the continuing Custis fortune owed its stability to his prudent and efficient management.

The years between his retirement and later re-emergence into public life were busy ones. He tried to make his estate self-supporting, as had his neighbor and friend, George Mason of Gunston Hall, but with little success. Ready cash was a rare commodity in the Virginia colony, and despite his business acumen he seldom succeeded in showing a profit. There were many complicated economic reasons for this; for example, English merchants refused to accept issues of colonial paper money. During the years of the Revolution and Washington's presidency, his overseers fell behind year after year. It is a credit to his stewardship that when he was in control he never fell behind.

Whenever he was in residence, there was the substantial added expense of entertainment to be reckoned. A constant stream of guests came to Mount Vernon for meals, for weekends, to go boating, to hunt foxes, to play cards. With all this he still found time to breed dogs, racehorses, and cattle, and to dabble in experimental agriculture. He also had a continued interest in public affairs. In 1758 he was re-elected to the House of Burgesses, and attended its meetings. This body was the first representative assembly in North America; it had been formed in 1619 to assist the governor in making laws and originating bills. When, in 1769, the Burgesses undertook to discuss the right and power of taxation, the governor hastily dissolved them. Unperturbed, however, they simply continued their meetings in the Raleigh Tavern, issuing all sorts of resolutions in defiance of executive authority.

Below: This engraving by Paul Revere of the "Boston Massacre" on March 5, 1770, had an enormous propaganda value. Actually it gives a somewhat prejudiced version of what really happened. There were only five killed, not seven, as the caption stated. The Redcoats, who were surrounded by an angry mob, lost their heads and fired despite the orders of their commander, Captain Preston, not to shoot. Brought to trial in Boston and defended by John Adams, among others, Preston and six of his men were acquitted. Two of the British received only light sentences.

THE ROAD
TO REVOLUTION

There are no real pauses in the course of history, but there are signposts which, certainly in retrospect, can be seen to point out the general direction. One of these was undoubtedly the Treaty of Paris, signed in 1763, which ended the French and Indian War in America and the Seven Years' War elsewhere. By one of its terms France lost Canada to England. Though it was an ironic twist of fate, from that moment on, England began to lose her 13 colonies. There is, however, a certain logic in this sequence. Britain was left the undoubted military victor, and she certainly ruled the waves, but she had incurred a staggering national debt and new obligations to patrol, not to say police, her new acquisitions. Not too unreasonably she decided that as the colonists would benefit from the protection of a British garrison, they should be required to contribute to its maintenance. It was estimated that the annual cost of this upkeep of 10,000 British regulars would come to £100,000, a sum greatly in excess of the annual revenue contributed by the 13 colonies to the mother country. The enforcement of old levies and the creation of new ones on the colonies seemed to be in order. But the colonists took instant and violent exception to any such move. It had been a time-honored practice for them to evade customs duties; indeed, the collection of royal customs was considered an amiable joke. The proposed enforcement gave rise to a gale of protests which, however loud, left London unmoved. There was also the added irritation of a proclamation issued by the king in 1763 forbidding any further encroachment by individuals or private land enterprises on the territory west of the Alleghenies. The measure was part of a large plan for the regulation of Indian affairs. The colonists were not only forbidden to settle on these lands; they were also prohibited from purchasing them from the Indians. If any land was to be bought from its rightful owners, it was to be done by king's representatives who were empowered to resell them to white settlers. The colonists considered that they had fought the French and Indian War to protect those very lands against the French for their own benefit. Had they fought in vain?

The bond between the parent nation and her colonies had been a slack one. The business community of London, the "City," had for some time taken a greater interest in them than had the Crown. In the eyes of the government, the colonies had served as a safety valve, an escape where could be sent, depending upon times and circumstances, malcontents and trouble-makers. The colonies did not yield much but neither did they cost very much. However, the Treaty of Paris changed this comfortable relationship. The business community and the government began to work in closer harmony, at the expense of harmony with their American posses-

sions. Long forgotten Acts of Trade and Navigation were revived, and long lists of taxable items made out. The one that pinched the hardest was the Sugar Act passed in 1764 which would have eaten into the profits derived from the processing of rum. Then came the Stamp Act which was passed by Parliament in 1765 without debate and certainly with no thought that it would be resisted, for it was a tax which Englishmen at home paid. But the uproar it caused in the colonies was almost unanimous: the newspapers, of which there were 30 odd, for once raised their voices in unison; in Williamsburg, Patrick Henry made an impassioned speech against it. Shortly thereafter came the Virginia Resolves, the first colonial answer to the Stamp Act, which stated firmly that only Virginians could tax Virginians. The Rhode Island Assembly adopted the Resolves in toto. Most of the other colonies also endorsed them. Then there were outbreaks of mob violence. The stamp distributor in Boston was made to resign, and the house of the lieutenant governor, Thomas Hutchinson, was wrecked, along with his priceless library. In New York the official coach of the lieutenant governor was burned, and the house of the commandant of the New York troops, Major James, was literally torn to pieces. Stamp distributors in the southern colonies were terrorized. The Great and General Court of Massachusetts sent out a ringing call for a Congress of all the colonies to meet in New York to consider collective action. Nine of the colonies sent representatives. It was an impressive assembly of distinguished men. The debate at first was noisy and discordant, but gradually they began to agree and finally accepted what must have seemed the expression of their own thoughts that: "There ought to be no more New England men, no New Yorkers . . . but all of us Americans!" The Congress produced a Declaration of Rights and Grievances which stated firmly, though respectfully, that only the colonies could levy taxes on the colonists. The following year the Stamp Act was repealed, for it had been proven impossible to enforce; business requiring the use of stamps was in part suspended, or simply carried on without their use. But the repeal of the act was accompanied by the passage of a statute affirming that the right to tax the colonies had always been the prerogative of the British government. Shortly thereafter the Townshend Acts were passed; these provided for the collection of taxes in the colonies on glass, lead, paper, paints and tea. They caused what must by now have seemed the inevitable outcry, and Boston merchants boycotted English goods. By 1770 the English government, discouraged by the colonists' uncooperative attitude and the financial loss to English merchants, repealed most of the acts except the one on tea. In order to help the financially em-

*Immediately below: The cartoon
drawn by Benjamin Franklin
which he sent to friends in 1767.
It describes the sad fate of
England if deprived of her
American colonies. Below:
another contemporary cartoon
shows the European powers
intent on stripping England
of all her wealth,
including her colonies.*

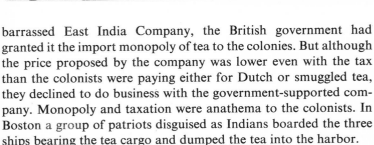

barrassed East India Company, the British government had
granted it the import monopoly of tea to the colonies. But although
the price proposed by the company was lower even with the tax
than the colonists were paying either for Dutch or smuggled tea,
they declined to do business with the government-supported company. Monopoly and taxation were anathema to the colonists. In
Boston a group of patriots disguised as Indians boarded the three
ships bearing the tea cargo and dumped the tea into the harbor.

As John Adams later pointed out, by now the "Revolution
was in the minds and hearts of the people." The series of acts
and laws which Parliament passed merely clarified the colonists'
thinking. Misunderstandings slowly grew into dissent, and then
dissidence which became open rebellion. The English unwittingly
did for their colonists what they could not do for themselves:
They succeeded in creating American unity, a seemingly impossible task, for the 13 colonies were in effect each separate and
independent. They were jealous of each other and hated each

other almost as much as they hated England. At this point, though,
these colonists realized that they were no longer English but
American. From then on the dialogue between England on the
one hand and America on the other was conducted between two
nations who shared the same mother tongue but gave different
meanings to the same words. They were, as George Bernard Shaw
said, two peoples divided by a common language.

Col. Isaac Barré, who had fought under the orders of General
Wolfe at the Battle of Quebec, and who had been a long-standing
friend of the colonists, speaking in Parliament, had described them
as "Sons of Liberty." It was the title chosen by the first secret
organizations to oppose the unpopular measures taken by the
British government. More often than not they were no more than
mobs, but initially there were genuine patriots among them. The
tug of war came to an end with the passage of the Intolerable
Acts in 1774 and the meeting in Philadelphia of the First Continental Congress.

Left: One of the
many prints inspired
by the Boston Tea Party
on December 11, 1773.
This one, published
in 1784, was done by
Daniel Chodowiecki,
a German painter
and engraver
born in Danzig
in 1726.

Below: This 1776 Whig cartoon
entitled "The Wise Men of Gotham
and their Goose" shows the
king's ministers about to behead
the goose that laid the golden
eggs—that is, the American
colonies. The cartoon was aimed
at the policy of force adopted
by King George III when, with
the appointment of Lord North
as head of the government,

every attempt at conciliation
came to an end. The "Wise Men
of Gotham" was an allusion to the
inhabitants of a village in
Nottinghamshire who had acquired
a reputation for doing ridiculous
things, probably to prevent
King John, in the 12th century,
from residing in the
town or building a highway
through it.

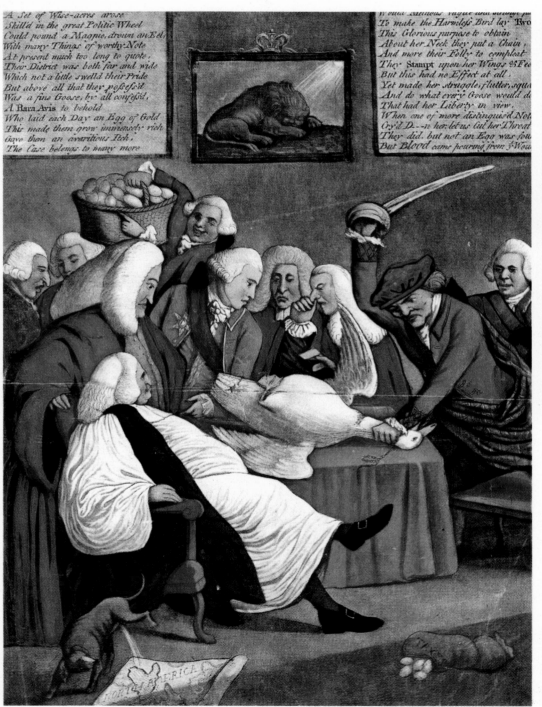

Above: Portrait by Allan Ramsay
of King George III, shown in
his coronation robes. In 1760,
at the age of 22, he succeeded
his grandfather. He was
the first of the Hanovers to be
born and brought up in England,
and he was determined to enforce
the rights of the Crown.
The frequent changes he brought
about in the government in
the years 1763 to 1770 gave
the American colonists the
impression that he was a hateful
tyrant determined to trample
upon their rights. Actually
his chief defect was weakness.

23

Below: "Tories put to the pillory," an English cartoon showing the burial of the Stamp Act. The law of March, 1765, which called for a seal to be put on documents and publications, was repealed the following year. The same fate had befallen the Sugar Act of 1764 which placed a duty on sugar and its derivatives, especially molasses. The repeal of these decrees was due in part to the damage they caused to English trade. Right: American contemporary cartoon of the "Tory Day of Reckoning." These were the Tories who had remained loyal to the British Crown. This drawing and others similar to it are proof of the rising aversion to English laws and to the agents responsible for their enforcement. The hostility gradually became more violent.

*Below: Thomas Paine, author
of* Common Sense, *which was
published in January, 1776.
The pamphlet produced a profound
change in everyone's thinking.
In America alone more than
100,000 copies of it were
distributed; the total output
ended up by being more than
500,000. It was the
first American bestseller.*

*Right: Peter Roshamel's painting
of Patrick Henry addressing the
Virginia House of Burgesses.
A lawyer and persuasive orator,
Patrick Henry was the mouthpiece
in Virginia of the young
frontier deputies who were
energetic pioneers as well. In
1765, when he was 29, he made his
famous condemnatory speech
against the king.*

Above: Franklin before the King's Privy Council as painted by Christian Schussele. Representative of the colonists in London and Postmaster General, Franklin was arraigned in 1774 for having released certain private letters written by the governor of Massachusetts, who thought restrictions ought to be imposed on "English liberties" in America. Copies of the letters were printed and circulated by Samuel Adams, without Franklin's knowledge, and used to incite revolt. Franklin was in many ways far ahead of his time. At a meeting in Albany in 1754 he had already put forth the first proposals of union among the colonies. His ideas had, at that time, seemed too radical. To the right: Copley's painting of the death of William Pitt, Earl of Chatham, who collapsed in the House of Lords on April 7, 1778, while making a speech denouncing the government's colonial policy. He died a few days later. His death deprived the colonists of a loyal supporter.

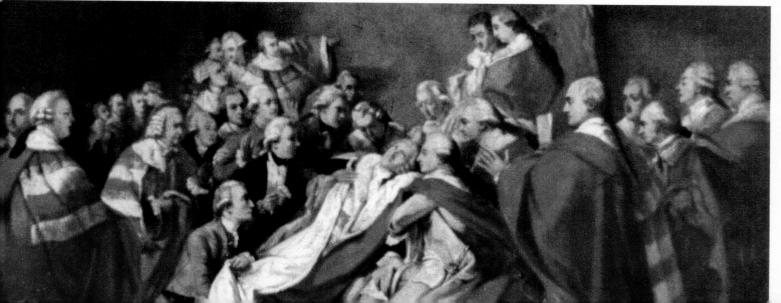

*Below: a view of Philadelphia
by Thomas Birch. At the outbreak
of the Revolution its inhabitants
already numbered 30,000.
Other principal American cities
were New York,
Charleston and Newport.*

THE FIRST CONTINENTAL CONGRESS

Directly below: The State House in Philadelphia, later known as Independence Hall, at the time of the First Continental Congress. The delegates, however, met in Carpenters' Hall. They were welcomed upon their arrival by the ringing of church bells. The city made a deep impression on many of them. Bottom of the page: The Congress Hall and New Theater in Philadelphia. Center: "The State of the English Nation," a cartoon drawn in 1778. At the right, a distraught Englishman is unable to arouse the sleeping British lion. Milking the cow, which represents England, are a Frenchman, a Dutchman and a Spaniard. An American is sawing off its horns.

The 50-odd delegates who met in Philadelphia from September 5 to October 26, 1774, represented 12 of the 13 colonies (Georgia did not participate until the Second Congress). They differed in origin, structure and internal administration. Seven of them, New Hampshire, New York, New Jersey, Virginia, North and South Carolina, and Georgia, were Crown colonies whose governors were appointed by the king. Maryland, Delaware and Pennsylvania were proprietary colonies where families like the Baltimores or the Penns chose the governors, with the king's approval. The last three, Massachusetts, Rhode Island, and Connecticut, were corporate colonies which chose their own governors, judges, assemblymen, councilors, juries and other officials. The New England and middle colonies possessed a thriving mercantile class and a well-balanced economy; the southern ones, which were chiefly engaged in agriculture, were already experiencing economic problems and were far more dependent on England than were the others. By its inept handling of colonial affairs, England managed in the decade 1765–1775 and especially with the passage of the Intolerable Acts, to unite even the most disparate geographical, professional, and social groups. The acts, four of which were passed to punish the people of Boston for the Boston Tea Party, contained the following provisions: the closing of the port of Boston until such time as the East India Company should be repaid for the tea destroyed in the affair; the changing of the Royal charter of Massachusetts; the forcing of the people of Massachusetts to quarter British troops sent there to enforce these measures; the granting to royal officials, in conflict with the colonial authorities, the right to trial in England. The Quebec Act, the last of the Intolerable Acts, caused almost as much of an uproar as had the Stamp Act. It was considered by the colonists to be a violation of the sea-to-sea grants of many colonial charters. It extended the boundaries of Quebec as far south as the Ohio River; it allowed the French Canadians to resume all the legal and political institutions they had under French rule; it guaranteed the Roman Catholic Church against any interference. In short, the provisions of the act would apply to the vast territory west of the Alleghenies which the colonists had been viewing with an acquisitive eye.

The purpose of the Congress, besides letting off steam, was to express colonial grievances against the English and to voice (and later implement) sentiments of solidarity with the citizens of Boston. Its chief tangible accomplishment was the creation of the Continental Association which forbade the importation and use of British goods and proposed the prohibition of colonial exports to England.

COMMANDER IN CHIEF

During the period between the First and Second Continental Congresses, October, 1774, to May, 1775, the political situation deteriorated further. The shooting had begun. In April a detachment of English soldiers had been sent to Concord to raid a cache of firearms and munitions. Minutemen, who had been alerted by Paul Revere on his famous ride, fired on them in Lexington—this was "the shot heard round the world." The British had returned the fire, killing eight colonists; they lost none of their own men. On the return march the British were again attacked, this time by a greater force, and would have been destroyed had not a relieving force been sent. The "Lexington alarm" served to mobilize an impromptu army of 20,000 to 30,000 farmers who came running to Boston. Some were in shirt-sleeves, others wore tag ends of ancient uniforms; there were cocked hats, beaver hats, red worsted caps. They carried old flintlocks, seven-foot guns, muskets which they loaded with scraps of iron or rusty nails in the absence of bullets. Powder horns hung at their sides. Officers were appointed, and the siege of Boston began. Meantime, British reinforcements were sent under the command of Generals Howe, Clinton and Burgoyne.

Feeling ran high throughout the colonies at the news of the outbreak of hostilities, greatly influencing the proceedings of the Second Continental Congress. The original intent of the delegates had been to consult with one another on the best means of co-operation against British trade; the state of war forced them into a union for purposes of defense. It was heartily endorsed by the New England delegates who, realizing that the army around Boston was primarily made up of volunteers from New England, feared it would be deserted by the other colonies. It was essential to gain the support of other sections. It was also of primary importance to appoint a commander in chief who would be acceptable to all factions. George Washington, one of the Virginia delegates, appeared from the very first meeting dressed in his uniform of colonel of the colonial militia, a uniform he had last worn in the honorable service of the Crown. He sat in Congress, silent, day after day. His silence as well as his uniform must have made him conspicuous in the assemblage of brilliant, indefatigable civilian speakers. His uniform was perhaps his way of saying that since war was inevitable he was ready to fight, a form of eloquence that must have seemed a blessed calm in the torrent of oratory. He was an experienced soldier, a wealthy aristocrat from the South, and seemed the ideal solution. When it was pointed out that perhaps a more democratic type of man would be more suitable, John Adams retorted that there was nothing the revolutionary movement needed quite so much as it needed aristocracy and wealth, and above all it needed a man who could rally Virginia, Georgia, Maryland and the Carolinas behind him. Accordingly, he nominated George Washington. The next day Washington was appointed unanimously. He made a modest speech of acceptance and refused to take any pay for his services. The gesture was effective and enhanced his prestige.

The Congress proceeded to pass some resolutions for the procurement of military supplies and the establishment of measures for the defense on the northern frontiers, the highlands of the Hudson and New York City.

Below: A Currier and Ives print of the appointment by the Continental Congress of Washington to the post of commander in chief. Standing before the members of Congress, Washington reads a brief statement. He refused the monthly salary of $500 assigned to him by the Congress, preferring to be reimbursed for his expenses. At the end of the war, which had lasted eight and a half years, he presented his bill, calculated to the last penny. The total came to about $64,000.

THE MAKING OF THE CONTINENTAL ARMY

Directly below: An engraving by Paul Revere showing the landing of the Redcoats in September 30, 1768. The English fleet had dropped anchor in Boston Harbor "as for a regular siege." The next day two regiments debarked at Long Wharf and "marched with insolent Parade" up King Street. Bottom of the page: A somewhat embellished version of Washington's assumption of his command in Cambridge on July 3, 1775. He had been expected on Sunday, July 2, but the arrangements for his welcome had to be canceled because of a violent rainstorm. He arrived in the afternoon and took command without any fanfare or formality.

Before leaving for Cambridge, the new commander in chief learned that the British had stormed and taken Bunker Hill. But he was reassured by the account he was given of the Americans' actions at the battle. The British won the day, but it had cost them almost half of the men engaged in the action. All of General Howe's staff were either killed or wounded; he himself never quite recovered from the horror of that battle. Until then British generals had had the utmost contempt for the Americans, thinking they would not fight. There was no place in British army tactics for the American style of fighting which was highly individualistic. The average American in the 1770's was a marksman without an equal in the rest of the world. To him war meant simply one thing: shooting someone. His one thought was to put a bullet where it ought to go, never mind about military formations. When a line of bayonets approached, he would run to cover and then fire again from behind trees or rocks. This made English officers assume he had no courage. The performance of the embattled farmers at Bunker Hill made them change their minds.

Nevertheless when Washington officially took over his command in Cambridge on July 3, 1775, there was little to cause him elation. The army he took over was New England's militia, which consisted of farmers, plowboys, backwoodsmen, countinghouse clerks, stevedores, all of whom were fighting a personal war. There was no discipline, a fact which was as galling to Washington as it was to the British. To the former they were a menace, swarming like bees to defend their hives and disappearing the moment the British had departed, whether in victory or defeat. They were truly "minutemen." They came from parts unknown, in a minute, and in another minute had disappeared. They were always present when provisions were distributed but disappeared when it was time for drill. Their lack of organization, discipline, *esprit de corps* beggars description. Each body of troops, being from a different colony, considered itself independent. They fraternized with the enemy and made no effort to separate officers from men. Furthermore they were there only on extremely short-term enlistments. This was the human material Washington had at his disposal. He fared even worse on money and supplies: lack of funds, no authority to raise any, a shortage of uniforms, stores, equipment, powder, ammunition.

It cannot be stressed too heavily that Washington was given no trained, regular army. He was always the amateur against the professional, always at the head of a dwindling army facing one whose sole business was fighting, and he was never supreme commander for very long. Congress made appointments and promotions of officers without consulting him.

THE BATTLE OF BUNKER HILL

BOSTON

This anonymous print of the fire in Charlestown describes one of the initial phases of the Battle of Bunker Hill (or Breed's Hill) on June 17, 1775. Charlestown juts out opposite Boston on a peninsula which closes one part of the bay. At the right of the print can be seen the Redcoats lined up to attack Bunker Hill, a small hill beyond the crest of Breed's Hill, whose profile stands out clearly to the right of the burning Charlestown houses. Bunker Hill had been occupied the day before by the Americans who were threatening Boston from the north. General Howe, who had recently replaced General Gage as commander in chief, gave the order to dislodge the Americans from the hill which had been hurriedly fortified by the insurgents. The frontal attack was conducted in three separate assaults. The hill was finally taken, but the English lost 1,054 men out of 2,300 used in the action. General Gage wrote after the battle that his losses were greater than he could again sustain. Among those who fell were James Abercromby, a colonel in the Grenadier Guards, and Major John Pitcairn of the Royal Marines. The consequences of that bloody battle considerably lowered the morale of the English expeditionary force.

Left: Trumbull's famous painting of the death of Dr. Joseph Warren at the Battle of Bunker Hill. A prominent Boston physician, Joseph Warren was only 34 when he was killed.
The painting also shows the fatally wounded Major Pitcairn being carried off the field.
The Americans were under the command of William Prescott, Richard Gridley, Israel Putnam and Thomas Knowlton. From the command post which had been hurriedly fortified, Prescott had ordered, "Don't fire until you can see the whites of their eyes."
The battle came to an end with furious hand-to-hand fighting. This was the real test by fire for the improvised militia.
Above: A contemporary English caricature satirizing victory by comparing it to the outlandish coiffures of the times. Right:
An episode at the Battle of Bunker Hill as shown in a German print.

THE CANNONS OF TICONDEROGA

Three weeks before the start of the war, it was decided that Fort Ticonderoga must be taken. Strategically the fort was of great importance as the key to the invasion route between Canada and the colonies. Accordingly at dawn on May 10, 1775, Ethan Allen and his Green Mountain Boys and a Connecticut colonel named Benedict Arnold surprised and defeated the tiny garrison of the fort. Allen awoke its commander by shouting, "Come out, you old rat!" After the Battle of Bunker Hill, Washington decided that the cannons must be brought to Boston and that "no Trouble or Expence must be spared to obtain them."

During the night of March 4, 1776, Washington occupied and fortified Dorchester Heights, overlooking Boston Harbor. On March 17, 1776, General Howe, who had long been preparing to shift the chief seat of war, evacuated the city and withdrew temporarily to Halifax. He took with him loyalist Bostonians who little thought they were never to return.

When the Congress had news of the British evacuation, there was justified rejoicing but also uncertainty. Where should the Americans concentrate their forces? They were not long left in the dark.

Left: Portrait of General Howe. Above: Trumbull's painting of the death of Montgomery. The Americans had tried to conquer Canada. The main column, led by Richard Montgomery, went up the St. Lawrence River Valley while Benedict Arnold's men followed another route. After exhausting marches and partial successes, Montgomery arrived in sight of Quebec, where he was joined by Arnold. The attack failed, and the death of Montgomery on December 31, 1775, marked the end of the undertaking. Right: Tom Lovell's painting "The Cannons of Ticonderoga." More fortunate than the attack on Quebec was the attack in March 1775 of Fort Ticonderoga on Lake Champlain. The cannons taken from the English were transferred to Boston.

INDEPENDENCE

Below: "The English leaving Boston" by M. A. Wageman. The departure was delayed by a hurricane, but it was accomplished without further trouble. Howe had threatened to set fire to the city if he was attacked. On March 17 the rebels entered the half-deserted city. Bottom of page: A meeting of the drafting committee of the Declaration of Independence. From left to right: Jefferson, Sherman, Franklin, Livingston and John Adams (standing). The task imposed upon them on June 11, 1776, by the Congress following a motion approved on June 7, was finished on July 1.

Meantime the Second Continental Congress continued in session. As the revolutionary movement gained momentum, executive authority in the royal and proprietary provinces collapsed; their assemblies were either dissolved or ceased to meet. The governors, their authority gone, either returned to England or found themselves prisoners. While the old system was collapsing, a new one was coming into being: There was a rise in the system of congresses, conventions and committees on a local level and on a "national" one. The Congress in Philadelphia met and issued bills of credit, regulated trade and Indian affairs, established postal communications. Richard Henry Lee, one of the Virginia delegates, introduced a resolution declaring "that these united colonies are and of right ought to be free and independent states." There was bitter opposition, but also enthusiastic support, and a drafting committee was set up to formulate a declaration of independence. After three weeks of work, mostly by Thomas Jefferson, the Declaration was passed by Congress on July 4, 1776. Even after the signing, dissention was still rampant, and Benjamin Franklin, bearing in mind the latest royal proclamation, was heard to declare mildly: "Gentlemen, we must all hang together now, or we shall assuredly all hang separately."

The Congress then turned its attention to the pressing problem of defending their new independence. The first step was the fortification of New York.

It was essential for the English to gain control of New York; its capture would provide not only an ideal harbor, but control of the Hudson River would provide a vital link in the water route to Canada. George Washington was well aware that British seizure of the city and its waterways would "stop the Intercourse between the northern and southern Colonies, upon which depends the safety of America." Consequently he hastily moved his army from Boston to the vicinity of New York and set up his headquarters there. But he made the mistake of splitting his army in two, stationing one half on Manhattan, the other half on Long Island. All the English had to do was to have their fleet, under the command of Admiral "Black Dick" Howe, brother of Gen. William Howe, sail up the East River to trap and destroy America's only army. But Sir William Howe delayed too long, as he was to do again and again. The battle of Long Island was fought on August 27, 1776, and lost by the Americans, who suffered 1,000 casualties, but Howe had failed to push his advantage, and his quarry slipped away under cover of a providential rain and fog. Quietly and quickly, Washington had had boats assembled, and in the course of the night he got his entire force across to Manhattan without the loss of another man. On November 16 Washington was forced to abandon New York State after the fall of Fort Washington where he lost 3,000 men.

Above: Caleb Boyle's portrait of
Jefferson. Thomas Jefferson
(1743-1826), who came from a
family of wealthy plantation owners,
was a delegate from Virginia to
the Congress and the author of
the Declaration of Independence.
As governor of Virginia in
1779 and 1780 he instituted
important reforms. After having
served two terms as President of
the United States, 1801-1809,
he retired to private life. Above
left: A tree of liberty erected
in honor of the Declaration of
Independence at noon on July 4,
1776. In Boston the mob burned
the royal coat of arms; in New York
it tore down the statue of
George III. Left: John Trumbull's
famous painting of the
official presentation of the
document to the Congress.

TWO VICTORIES: TRENTON AND PRINCETON

At the end of 1776 Washington's forces had dwindled down to 3,500 men. Immediately after the defeat on Long Island he had retreated to New Jersey hotly pursued by the energetic Cornwallis. Congress, meantime thinking Philadelphia would be captured, fled to Baltimore, but they had at last given Washington freedom to act.

Howe, who had settled his troops in their winter quarters instead of driving Washington's forces to some remote place of refuge, had returned to New York. Before doing this he had set up a chain of posts in New Jersey at Newark, Amboy, New Brunswick, Princeton, and Trenton; his theory was that no army ever campaigned in the winter. Cornwallis prepared to go on home on leave. Clinton sailed off to enjoy Newport, and winter closed down on the Delaware.

Washington, who had put the river between himself and the enemy, recrossed it and on December 26 surprised the Hessians who were encamped at Trenton. The crossing had been a difficult one: There were blocks of ice floating on the current, and it was raining and sleeting so hard that muskets could not be used because of wet powder. He ordered his men to use bayonets. At eight A.M. they fell upon the unsuspecting 1,500 Hessians whose commander was sleeping off his Christmas wine, captured some 900 of them, and themselves lost only four men. The attack lasted less than 45 minutes.

The news of the Trenton victory electrified the colonies and recharged the army's morale. The British high command was staggered and canceled Cornwallis's leave, rushing him with 8,000 well-clothed, well-equipped men to Princeton. The American forces were almost trapped, but they managed to slip out, routed the British force at Princeton and finally took up winter quarters at Morristown. The Americans were fought out, but they had brought hope to a seemingly hopeless cause.

One cannot too often repeat the appalling conditions under which the men fought—shoeless, half-naked many of them, in want of blankets, food, ammunition. And yet they persevered.

The retreat from Long Island was accomplished during the night of August 29, 1776, under a protecting mantle of fog. Thanks also to the expert skill of the Salem mariners 9,500 soldiers along with their baggage and equipment reached the other bank of the Hudson at Manhattan. The English took only three prisoners who had stayed behind to loot. They did not make the most of the victory which they had won two days before. Far left: "Washington leaves Long Island" by M. A. Wageman. Left: The artillery transported to the opposite shore. Above: A painting by J. W. Dunsmore of Washington and his generals making plans after the defeat of Long Island. The English forces concentrated in New York included 30 warships and 400 transport ships, 32,000 soldiers and 10,000 sailors. The American troops retreated to the south across New Jersey. In three months Washington lost 5,000 men taken prisoner. Among these was General Lee, captured on December 13 by the soldiers of the regiment in which he had served during the French and Indian War.

43

WASHINGTON CROSSING THE DELAWARE

This well-known painting is by Emanuel Leutze. Born in Germany in 1816, Leutze emigrated to Philadelphia with his parents 14 years later. It was here that he took his first art courses. He worked in Washington and New York, and then in 1841 he left America for Europe where he settled in Düsseldorf as a pupil of Karl Friedrich Lessing whose influence led him to paint historical episodes, a style of painting much in vogue in Germany at the time. After having studied in Munich and in Italy, where he painted a number of pictures that met with great success, Leutze executed the work destined to celebrate Washington's feat. It was exhibited in the United States Capitol in 1851. Its success brought the painter back to the United States, where he was commissioned to decorate the Capitol in Washington. "Washington Crossing the Delaware" was reproduced many times, though his romantic interpretation of a crucial moment in the War of Independence has a dramatic impact that is hardly equaled by its esthetic value. Washington succeeded in ferrying to the other side of the river, held by Hessian troops in the service of the English, 24,000 men and 18 cannons. The American losses were minimal: four killed, two of whom were frozen to death.

Cornwallis, who rushed forward with reinforcements of 8,000 men after Trenton, thought the fox was in the bag. But Washington turned on him and defeated him again at Princeton on January 3, 1777. *Left:* Two details in Trumbull's painting of the battle: the death of General Mercer. Princeton, after Trenton, did much to improve American morale. *Below:* "The American artillery in action at Princeton," an eye-witness painting by William Mercer, a son of the general killed in the battle. *Far below:* "The Surrender of the Hessians at Trenton" by John Trumbull (1756-1843). He was famous for his paintings of historical subjects which were always carefully documented. He also served as one of Washington's aides and later pursued a brief diplomatic career.

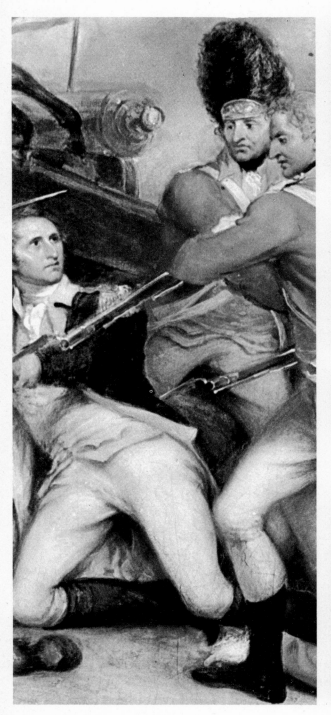

SARATOGA

In London, in the spring of 1777, the colonial secretary, Lord George Germain, made a plan for an invasion from Canada in which Tories and Indians were to take part. Since the Indians had scalped the Anglo-Americans for the French, why not use them again against the Americans? Gen. Sir John Burgoyne (Gentleman Johnny) was to come down from Canada. Sir William Howe was to proceed along the valley of the Hudson to meet him in Albany. Once their forces were joined, the game would be up. But the plan was doomed from the outset by the neglect of British officials to send General Howe his instructions. The two English commanders, Burgoyne in the north and Howe in the south, pursued their own separate ways. Things went badly for Burgoyne against whom a contingent under the command of General Gates had been sent. Burgoyne awaited, in vain, the reinforcements which were supposed to arrive from New York with General Clinton. His troops, reduced to 6,000, were defeated by Gates's 9,000 at Freeman's Farm on September 19. Burgoyne retreated into the fort at Saratoga, 30 miles north of Albany, and there, surrounded by the Americans, surrendered on October 17, 1777. In one single battle the English had lost a quarter of their troops and an important line of communication. The surrender of an entire British army with all its equipment gave a tremendous psychological boost to the Americans.

Things went better for Howe. He first tried and failed to draw Washington into an open battle. Then he withdrew to New York where he embarked 15,000 men and headed out to sea. For a moment Washington feared he would go to Boston, which was undefended. A month later Howe landed on the Chesapeake Bay, 50 miles from Philadelphia. He defeated Washington at Brandywine Creek on September 11, 1777, but it was by no means a decisive victory. The American army was still ready and able to fight again, which it did on October 4 at Germantown. Although the British also won this battle, Washington and his men were not discouraged for they had nearly won the field. The fierce fighting by the American troops did not go by unnoticed in France, which was always ready to tweak the tail of the British Lion. Washington blockaded Philadelphia, occupied by the British, thereby forcing Howe to call for help of the Royal Navy in opening the Delaware to supply ships. Washington finally had to retreat but not before costing the British one 64-gun ship, one sloop and three badly cut up battalions of Hessian grenadiers.

Howe settled in for a comfortable winter in Philadelphia which Congress had hastily abandoned; there were receptions, banquets and balls to help while away the time. Washington settled his men a few miles outside of Philadelphia in Valley Forge for their winter quarters. It was, as he wrote with his customary economy of words, "a dreary kind of place and uncomfortably provided."

Far left: Two English cartoons expressing English scorn for the surrender of General Burgoyne at Saratoga on October 17, 1777, and for General Howe's inactivity. Saratoga marked the end of the English attempt to cut the colonies in two. Two columns had gone from Canada. The first, which followed the St. Lawrence and went beyond Lake Ontario, attacked from the west in order to open up the way to Albany. It was pushed back to Fort Stanwix by the Americans under Arnold. Burgoyne, who commanded the second column, came down along Lake Champlain and Lake George and found his left flank unprotected. Beaten twice at Freeman's Farm on September 19 and October 7, he retired to Fort Saratoga but was forced to surrender after an unsuccessful attempt to get out. Above: Arnold (on the white charger) attacks the English at Freeman's Farm as Gen. Sir Simon Fraser is carried off the field. Left: Trumbull's painting of Burgoyne surrendering his sword to General Gates (in white).

Above: Caricature of General Lee. English-born Charles Lee was an experienced officer who was appointed major general by the Congress. An arrogant, difficult man, he looked upon himself as the equal of Washington, often ignoring his orders. Freed by the English after 16 months in prison, he was given back his command, which Washington deprived him of at Monmouth on June 28, 1778. Left: "Battle of Germantown" by Alonzo Chappel. Germantown, five miles from Philadelphia, was the scene, on October 4, 1777, of Washington's frontal attack against the British forces. Two American columns collided in a blinding fog and fired on each other; precious time was wasted by another element in trying to capture the Chew mansion which was like a fortress. Despite their defeat the Americans gave a good account of themselves.

Below, left: Uniforms of the Continental Army (1776–1779). Directly below: American troops at Valley Forge. At the beginning of the winter, Washington found himself with greatly reduced forces partly through desertions and partly through the expiration of enlistments. On paper the total was 60,000 men. In actual fact, it was 11,000. The commander in chief was authorized to enlist directly an army which took the name of "continental." It consisted of 16 battalions of infantry, three regiments of artillery, 3,000 cavalrymen and foot soldiers. With this instrument of war, small but efficient, Washington came through the frightful winter of Valley Forge.*

Left: Betsy Ross puts together the first American flag. The story is that she ran a shop on Arch Street in Philadelphia and had been commissioned to make one in June, 1776, by Washington himself. It was supposed to have been her suggestion that five-pointed stars rather than six-be chosen. Actually the Congress adopted the Stars and Stripes only on June 14, 1777. The story of Betsy Ross, although widespread, is not based on solidly proven historical facts. The first written version of it dates from 1870. Above, right: *Baron Friedrich von Steuben, who was recommended by Benjamin Franklin, became the drillmaster of the American forces at Valley Forge. A former Prussian captain under Frederic II—and not a general as he boasted of having been—he did a superb job. Another of the noted foreigners who came rushing to American aid was Tadeusz Kosciuszko (right). The future Polish national hero soon became a commander in the Engineers where he distinguished himself.*

VALLEY FORGE

Certain place names have become symbols. Valley Forge is one of ours; it stands for misery and endurance. Washington had little to say in the selection of this site for his winter quarters. Political pressure forced him to remain in Pennsylvania whereas he would have preferred Wilmington. The main column of his army reached Valley Forge on the afternoon of December 19, 1777, in a freezing rain after traveling along deeply rutted roads that tore at rag-bound feet and sent baggage carts astray. He later wrote, "You might have tracked the army . . . to Valley Forge by the blood of their feet." It was not only clothing that was lacking: blankets, food and shelter were likewise in short supply. It was so bitterly cold that tents were useless. Accordingly the men were put to work building log huts and sent out on foraging expeditions because the farmers and neighboring inhabitants were unwilling to make any contributions to the upkeep of the army. Of the 11,000 men who arrived in December, barely 6,000 remained—some 2,500 had died, the other 2,500 had deserted. But despite the ravages of disease, malnutrition and exposure, the army held together and survived the winter.

The reflection that the British were living warmly and gaily in Philadelphia and that the people of Pennsylvania were enjoying all the comforts of a rich countryside must have been galling to the shivering, starving army. But with his customary fortitude Washington endured everything: the justified grumbling of his men, harsh and unfair public criticism, and the captious meddling by a Congress too weak to help him. He did point out to them in a letter:

> I can assure those gentlemen, that it is a much easier and less distressing thing to draw remonstrances in a comfortable room by a good fireside, than to occupy a cold, bleak hill, and sleep under frost and snow, without clothes or blankets. However, although they seem to have little feeling for the naked and distressed soldiers, I feel superabundantly for them, and, from my soul, I pity those miseries, which it is neither in my power to relieve or prevent.

It was at this low point that his political enemies chose to hatch a plot to dislodge him. Involved in it were Thomas Conway, Gen. Horatio Gates, Gen. Charles Lee and a number of others. Among them also were some congressmen whose antagonism sprang from factional jealousies between the North and the South rather than from personal animosity. Even John

Adams, whose candidate he had been, had second thoughts about him. It is an everlasting tribute to Washington's generosity that he never allowed the memory of this plot against him to affect his subsequent relations with the men involved.

In spite of all the difficulties, by the time spring had come, his army was better disciplined, better trained than it had ever been before. And when on May 6, 1778, word reached him that the French had decided to come to his aid, he was considerably cheered. The French never lost a chance to oppose the English, and this seemed a heaven-sent way of getting revenge for their defeat in the Seven Years' War. Furthermore they had been impressed by Washington's successes as well as by the manner of his defeats. Benjamin Franklin's popularity in Paris and his diplomatic skill disguised under a simple rustic exterior did much to hasten French interest in helping the American cause.

FRENCH INTERVENTION

The intervention of the French in the spring of 1778 changed the face of the war. What had started as a family quarrel took on the aspects of world war. It was, as usual with the British, a predominantly commercial and naval conflict.

General Howe, accused of having simply run aground in Philadelphia, was replaced by Sir Henry Clinton. The latter went back to the original plan of using New York as the center of operations since the capture of the rebel capital had proven a failure, probably because there wasn't yet enough of a government to make it worthwhile. Clinton's chief problem was to get his army to New York. Afraid of the possible arrival of a French fleet, he dared not move it by sea. Accordingly he marched through New Jersey, pursued by Washington's army which was now in good shape. According to a French historian, Washington's strategy was to have none; he limited himself for a while to sniping at the British rear guard. But at Monmouth he ordered an immediate attack. Gen. Charles Lee, who was not given to instant and blind obedience, delayed until it was almost too late. Fortunately, just as he had ordered his troops to retreat, Washington arrived at full gallop, rallied the retreating Americans, and in one of his rare bursts of temper, fired Lee on the spot. Lee was later court-martialed but got off with a light sentence. Thanks to Lee's dilatoriness the British forces were able to withdraw to New York in good order with their wagon train intact.

The following month the French, who had undertaken to provide troops, ships and supplies to their new ally, sent an expeditionary force under Admiral d'Estaing; it was not a success. In 1780 a second one consisting of 55,000 men, led by the Comte de Rochambeau, at least succeeded in establishing good relations between the allies. The people of Newport, where the French were stationed, at first viewed their arrival with alarm. It was short-lived; the French paid for everything with gold. Rochambeau's army must have been the most perfectly disciplined one ever seen on this continent. During the year that they remained not one single impropriety was reported; not one chicken, not one apple was stolen.

Meantime, Washington had taken up his headquarters at West Point in order to keep an eye on Clinton's movements. He was still hampered by a Congress too weak to support him, by popular discouragement and a mutinous army which was as always underfed and underequipped. The English, lured with hopes that the southern loyalists would welcome them with open arms, and thinking that with control of the seas they could easily transfer troops from the West Indies to Carolina, shifted the center of operations to the south.

YORKTOWN

Below: Pennsylvania's Wyoming Massacre by Alonzo Chappel. The episode occurred during the campaign conducted in the south by the English, the Tories and their Indian allies in the summer of 1778. Indian atrocities were useful to American propaganda.

The outlook for the Americans was again bleak. Savannah had been captured in December, 1778; on May 12, 1780, Charleston fell to the British. On August 18, 1780, General Gates, the hero of Saratoga, was ignominiously defeated at Camden, S.C. In September, Benedict Arnold turned traitor and passed to the English side. However, the British hope of detaching Georgia and the Carolinas from the American cause was foiled by their mishandling of their potential allies and by the type of hit-and-run fighting against which they continued to be helpless. Nathanael Greene, who had taken over Gates's command of the southern army, turned the tide with the help of Daniel Morgan, "Light-Horse" Harry Lee, and the leaders of the partisan bands, Marion, Sumter and Pickens. He pressed the British forces so hard that they were forced to retreat. Clinton ordered Cornwallis who was "quite tired of marching about the country" to pull back his forces to a Chesapeake port where he could send him reinforcements.

In June, the French forces that had spent such a pleasant year in Newport marched down to join Washington's men along the Hudson. Again French discipline on the march and in camp aroused general admiration. The French themselves were impressed with General Washington personally and especially with his methods of shifting his forces to conceal their true size.

In August, 1781, Washington and Rochambeau received word that Admiral de Grasse, with 28 ships of the line and additional troops in transport ships, had cleared the French West Indies. Washington decided that American and French forces were to proceed south at once to join Lafayette and Wayne. Their massed forces could be thrown against Cornwallis who was dug in at Yorktown. Time was of the essence; so was money. Rochambeau offered Washington half of the gold left in his military chest. The American contingent led the way, gathering strength. When they arrived in Williamsburg, there were 9,800 Frenchmen and Americans. The total swelled gradually to an impressive 16,000. On September 15, 1781, word came that Admiral de Grasse had met the British fleet, defeated it and closed the sea approaches to Yorktown; also Admiral Barras who had left Newport with the heavier French ordinance and tons of salt beef for the armies was safe and heading for anchorage in the James River. Meantime, the heavy guns were emplaced along the river; the Marquis de Choisy pushed his lines right up to the British works, and the British forces were bottled up completely. On October 17, after days of

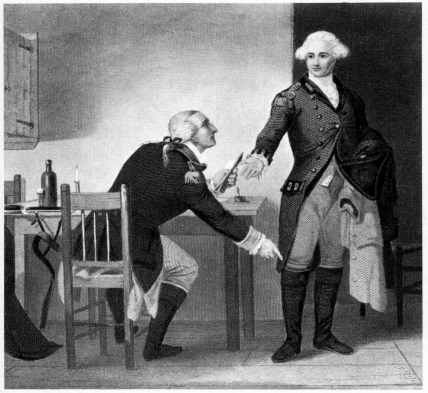

heavy cannonade, the British asked for peace parleys. Two days later General O'Hara, deputy for Cornwallis, surrendered to General Benjamin Lincoln, deputy for Washington. That same night the commander in chief drafted a characteristically modest report to inform Congress of victory. It was worded in such a way that credit for the success was given to "every Officer and Soldier in the combined Army in this Occasion."

To all intents and purposes the war was over. The English evacuated Charleston and Savannah and remained inactive in New York for two years. The formal peace treaty was finally signed on September 3, 1783, eight-and-a-half long, bitter years after that first volley had been fired on Lexington Green. In November the British troops embarked on their transports and set sail; early in December the American army, led by Henry Knox, entered New York. On December 4, Washington bade his officers a laconic and moving farewell. On December 23 he went to Annapolis, where Congress was in session, to submit his resignation, present his bill for expenses, and commend to their attention the soldiers and officers who had served for two years, almost without pay. Mutiny had been spreading even among the officers. He had appeared before the discontented ones with a paper in his hand and taking out his glasses had said simply: "You see, Gentlemen, I have grown both blind and gray in your service." The revolt subsided. Eventually they collected some back pay, but the Congress was slow in allowing it.

Left: Eugene Lami's painting of one of the assaults conducted at Yorktown on the night of October 14, 1783. The Americans, led by Alexander Hamilton, overwhelm the Red coats and raise the Stars and Stripes in a gesture which was echoed in the sculpture of the Marines at Iwo Jima. Lower left: Benedict Arnold's betrayal.

The general, seated at the table, points out to his accomplice the boot where the plans of West Point were to be hidden. Arnold, the hero of Saratoga, sold himself to the enemy for £6315. Found out, he made good his escape, but died in exile years later, forgotten and despised.

Above: Hamilton, in the trenches at Yorktown. Alexander Hamilton (1757–1804) emigrated in 1773 to America from the West Indies, where he was born, and became one of the active supporters of American independence. One of Washington's youngest aides, he distinguished himself by his qualities of leadership and his courage. He later became a staunch supporter of the Federalists, i.e., of a strong central government. He said that confederation was good neither for peace nor for war. He opposed Jefferson and was killed in a duel provoked by Aaron Burr.
Left: Washington with Lafayette and his aide Tench Tilghman at Yorktown by Charles Willson Peale. In 1781 Lafayette, who was then 22 years old, had a command of his own in the south.

57

Left: "The surrender of Cornwallis at Yorktown" by John Trumbull. At the right is Washington followed by his staff. The two men in the center are the Irish General O'Hara and the American General Benjamin Lincoln who accepts the surrender. Lord Cornwallis had sent word he was indisposed.

UNEASY BEGINNINGS

There were now Americans but as yet no America. The peace treaty with England listed separately the 13 states, successors to the 13 colonies. The Declaration of Independence did not imply union among 13 small independent countries, merely a league of friendship. The tie that bound the states was tenuous and had been good only for the duration of the war. Now that the war was over the bond was practically dissolved. Josiah Tucker, dean of Gloucester and one of England's leading economic and political authorities, predicted that we had no future: "The mutual antipathies and clashing interests of the Americans, their difference of governments, habitudes, and manners, indicate that they will have no centre of union and no common interest. They never can be united into one compact empire under any species of government whatever." The Articles of Confederation, adopted in 1781, made a contribution to the techniques of government by setting up a Congress and apportioning taxes; they did not establish national unity and before long proved wholly unsatisfactory because of the subordinate position they gave the central government. Under their provisions, Congress was forbidden to engage in wars, negotiate treaties or alliances, or coin money without the consent of a majority of the states. They also stipulated that the articles were to be unanimously ratified by the states and that no alterations could be made unless agreed to by Congress and by the legislature of every state. When it became apparent, as it soon did, that government under the Articles of Confederation was, as George Washington said, "little more than the shadow without the substance," agitation for a stronger government began.

Meantime, George Washington had returned to his estates, eager to devote much of his time and energies to agriculture and to the recouping of his dwindling assets. His losses during the war had been substantial. He now embarked on all sorts of horticultural experiments, enlarged the Mount Vernon house and laid out the grounds anew.

He did not lose sight of public affairs. He pointed out to his friends early in 1786 that the political plight of the United States was such that "something must be done, or the fabric must fall, for it is certainly tottering." Later he wrote, "I do not conceive that we can exist long as a nation without having lodged somewhere a power which will pervade the whole union in as energetic a manner as the authority of the state government extends over the several states." Finally a convention of all the states was called in Philadelphia in May, 1787.

Above, left: "Washington Taking
Leave of His Generals," by Alexander
Ritchie. The very simple
ceremony took place in Queen's
Head Tavern belonging to Samuel
Fraunces, a staunch patriot of West
Indian birth. He later sold the
tavern and became the steward
of Washington's household. Above:
Benjamin West's painting of the
signing of the peace treaty between
England and her former colonies.
The artist started with portraits
of the American delegates who
were, left to right, John Jay,
John Adams, Benjamin Franklin,
Henry Laurens and Franklin's
grandson, William Temple Franklin,
secretary to the American
delegation. The English refused
to pose when their turn came so
the painting was never completed.
Left: Washington's entrance
into New York.

59

A MORE PERFECT UNION

Fifty-five delegates from 12 states (Rhode Island ignored the call) met, ostensibly to amend the Articles of Confederation, but they soon realized the impossibility of effectively patching a document so inherently unsound in principle. The articles were scrapped, and a wholly new document was drafted. By mid-September, 1787, the Federal Convention had adjourned, its task completed. The next step was to get the Constitution ratified by the various state legislatures. Nine states, the required majority, had done so before the end of June, 1788, and the Constitution was declared the fundamental law of the United States. Rhode Island finally fell into line in 1790 after a threat that it would be treated as a foreign country and a string of customhouses set up along her borders.

Washington presided over the deliberations of the drafting of the Constitution, which lasted for four months. In the four months he spoke up only once as a delegate, and then it was on a minor question of congressional apportionment. But though he said little in debate, he did much to insist on clearly defined powers. He did not believe the final document to be perfect, but his support helped push it through the Virginia legislature, and a letter in which he wrote "it or dis-union is before us to chuse from" that was published in a Boston newspaper did much to influence the Massachusetts legislature.

Far left: Regnier's lithograph showing Washington as gentleman farmer. Washington had acquired Mount Vernon in 1752 at the death of his eldest brother's daughter (Lawrence himself had died the same year). He left it in the care of his brother John Augustine (Jack) during the French and Indian War. During the Revolution a distant relative administered the estate for him. In the space of 45 years Mount Vernon increased from 2,126 acres to over 8,000 acres. Left: C. W. Peale's portrait of Martha Washington. Below: "The Cincinnatus of America in 1783" by J. L. Ferris celebrates the return of the commander in chief to private life. A society of the Cincinnati, made up of a number of former officers in the War of Independence, gave its name to the city in Ohio which was founded in 1788.

Below: "Washington's Silver Wedding Anniversary" by J. L. Ferris. The former commander in chief is shown, with his wife by his side, welcoming their guests to Mount Vernon. When, in 1759, he had married Martha and settled down with her and her two children by a former marriage, Washington wrote to a friend: "I believe I have settled with an amiable wife for the remainder of my life and hope to find in my retirement more happiness than I have ever found in a large and troubled world."

THE CONSTITUTION

Having discarded the Articles of Confederation and decided to set up a workable system of government, the delegates immediately found themselves divided on the makeup of the new Congress. The smaller states, wishing to retain their power, wanted equal representation in the Congress; the larger states, wishing to have power fall where population and wealth lay, wanted proportional representation. It was decided, after much bitter debate, to set up a lower house, to be elected according to population (the House of Representatives), and an upper house in which the states would have equal representation (the Senate). After this initial compromise the way was relatively easy. There were clear lines of demarcation between the three branches of the government: the executive, the legislative and the judiciary. The Constitution is a concise one, consisting of a preamble and seven articles. Its very brevity has left it open to reinterpretation in changing times. Although the preamble confers no power, it has been important because of the words used. For example, "We, the people of the United States" has been used by the supporters of a strong federal union in opposition to the proponents of states' rights; "to . . . promote the general Welfare" has been the basis for much social legislation.

Within two years the Bill of Rights, consisting of nine amendments, had been added because it was felt that there was insufficient guarantee of individual liberties, and it was for individual liberties that, to a great extent, the war had been fought.

Although often referred to as a revolution, the conflict was really a war of independence. Revolution implies the upset, as it did in France in 1789 and in Russia in 1917, of classes, manners, customs and all ways of life; our fight against the British merely threw them out. The last thing the delegates in Philadelphia wanted was to upset the economic and social *status quo*.

Just as Washington had seemed the perfect choice as commander in chief, so again he seemed to fulfill the requirements for President. He alone commanded the respect of all regional factions and of the two parties to which the struggle over the ratification had given rise. His prestige in Europe was unequaled by any other American, even Franklin. He was unanimously elected first President of the United States. As he was a southerner, it was thought wise to choose a northerner as Vice President. This choice was not so clear-cut, but John Adams received the most votes and was duly elected to serve with Washington.

THE FIRST PRESIDENT

Below: The Arch of Triumph erected in Philadelphia on April 20, 1789, in honor of the new President. A special device had been set up to drop a crown of laurels on Washington's head as he went under the arch. Washington's progress from Mount Vernon to New York was a triumphal march. He was inaugurated at New York amid universal rejoicing.

Right: Washington taking the oath of office on April 30, 1789, on the balcony of Federal Hall in New York which was the first seat of the government. Far right: T. H. Matteson's painting of Washington delivering the Inaugural Address. In this first speech the new President outlined in general the function of the government, thus placing himself above various factions. Shortly after having assumed office, Washington made a nationwide trip. He first visited the northern states, then the southern ones, showing an interest in their particular problems. Growing industries also received his support. From the time he became President, Washington always wore clothes manufactured in America, a fact proudly announced by the newspapers.

The first Congress was supposed to meet on March 4, 1789, but the House did not have a quorum until April 2, and the Senate did not organize until April 5. On April 6 the electoral votes were counted, and Washington and John Adams were announced as President and Vice President. Before setting forth from Mount Vernon to New York, Washington had to borrow money for the trip and for his initial expenses. Although he was considered a wealthy man he was land-poor and was always hard up for ready cash.

On April 30, near the spot now marked by Ward's statue of him in Wall Street, he took the oath of office before a cheering crowd.

Early in his first term, Washington, who by breeding and natural inclination had always been minutely careful of the proprieties, established firm rules of behavior for the President. He recognized the importance of outward form and carefully defined the limits between himself as a public personage and as a private man. A lengthy debate on the title he should adopt was resolved by the choice of the simplest possible form of address: The President of the United States.

In both New York and Philadelphia he rented the best houses available. He had refused the hospitality of the Governor of New York, George Clinton, believing that the head of the nation ought not to be a long-term guest. He drove in a coach accompanied by four outriders in rich livery and drawn by a team of either four or six horses. At receptions he wore a black velvet suit, gold buckles on his shoes, yellow gloves and a sword in a white leather scabbard. One day of the week was set aside for all persons wishing to see him; on other days special appointments had to be set up. When the government moved to Philadelphia, Mrs. Washington held a reception every Friday afternoon at which the President often appeared. He chatted with everyone, but never very gaily. He was described as being "invariably grave; it was a sobriety that stopped short of sadness." The Revolution had taken something from him and "he had become gray inside" as well as out.

THE BIRTH OF POLITICAL PARTIES

Washington's Administration was marked by the same caution, methodical precision and sober judgment he had always shown. The function of a good executive is to select men who are highly skilled for the work in hand, and he had a talent for picking talented men who could do their work effectively. His first cabinet was made up of four men: Thomas Jefferson as Secretary of State, Alexander Hamilton as Secretary of the Treasury, Henry Knox as Secretary of War, and Edmund Randolph as Attorney General. In selecting them, he balanced the two newly formed parties evenly.

The country had drifted slowly into one or the other of two opposing political divisions: the Federalist Party and the Democratic Party. The Federalists were followers of Hamilton, conservatives devoted primarily to the interests of wealthy land owners and businessmen and were fervent supporters of a strong central government. They advocated the strengthening of the union at the expense of the states. Henry Knox belonged to this group. The other one, the Jeffersonians, at first called themselves Anti-federalists, then Democratic-Republicans, then Democrats. To this party belonged some wealthy plantation owners, but in the main it was made up of the common people—small farmers, little merchants and workingmen. They were proponents of states' rights and looked upon the United States as a league of sovereign states that had delegated a few of their powers and rights to a federal authority. Jefferson and his followers opposed the tariff, the rich aristocracy and any kind of class privilege. Edmund Randolph belonged to this party.

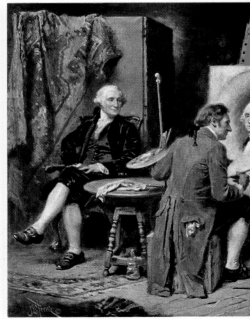

Washington conceived of the Presidency as holding itself aloof from all factions. By his choices he had achieved a perfect, if delicate, balance. It fell to his lot to cast the deciding vote in any controversial issue. By and large, however, he leaned more heavily toward Hamilton, supporting his scheme for the assumption of state debts, establishing the United States Bank and in general strengthening the authority of the Federal Government.

Far left: Gilbert Stuart's portrait of Washington. Left: "The artist and the President" by J. L. Ferris. Washington had become so tired of posing for painters that in a letter to a friend dated 1785 he said he had become "a monument to Patience." Many portraits of him were done by the two Peales, Charles Willson and his son Rembrandt. The most famous one, done by Stuart, was turned down by Martha Washington because she said that it looked unfinished. Right: Copley's portrait of John Adams (1735–1826), our first Vice President who held a number of diplomatic posts as well. Above: Daniel Huntington's painting of a reception held by Martha Washington. A number of radical opponents of the Federalists accused Washington of behaving like a king. One of the most vociferous of these was Philip Freneau, a clerk in the State Department under Jefferson. Fine wines and good food were served at the presidential table, but some of the guests, like Senator Maclay, complained that the atmosphere was too solemn. Actually Washington insisted upon having the receptions as informal as possible. The "solemnity" which they reproached him with was more due to his instinctive reserve than to any excessive importance attributed by him to his position.

TROUBLED YEARS

WASHINGTON AND HIS CABINET.

The idyll between country and Congress on the one hand and the President on the other was not destined to last. After his first term, Washington was again reelected unanimously, but new situations gave rise to new problems. The French Revolution, after having been at first strongly influenced by the American one, was turning into a carnage. Our own economic problems were growing acute, and political theories were filling the air. The political parties were becoming clearly defined, and the struggle among the differing currents was becoming more bitter. Democrats and Federalists were hardly civil to each other. Times were indeed changing, and in his second term Washington held less control. Toward the end of 1793 Jefferson resigned as Secretary of State. His constant clashes with Hamilton and his disapproval of the refusal by the United States to honor the treaty of alliance with France precipitated his action. Hamilton's view was that the United States was so beset with its own economic and administrative problems that it could not embroil itself in another war (France was again at war with England). The excuse given was that our treaty had been made with Louis XVI who had since been guillotined. Washington, keenly aware of the United States Govern-

ment's precarious position, supported Hamilton. Other serious troubles arose. In 1794 he ordered the repression of the Whiskey Rebellion staged by the farmers of Western Pennsylvania who objected to an excise tax. Hamilton had imposed the tax in 1791. The rebellion was quelled without bloodshed, and the prisoners taken were pardoned by Washington, but the hatred engendered by the Federalists did not abate for many years. The next source of trouble was Jay's treaty concluded in 1794 with Great Britain to settle the difficulties arising out of violations of the Treaty of Paris in 1783 and to regulate commerce and navigation. The terms of the treaty, particularly those dealing with the rights of American seamen and with international maritime laws, aroused a storm of indignation. Jay was denounced and burned in effigy. Hamilton, speaking in its defense, was struck by a stone. He commented, "If you use such striking arguments, I must retire." He did. From the Cabinet as well. Washington had lost two able but diametrically opposed aides. With them gone, the spotlight fell on him, and he was an easy target. There was a torrent of abuse poured on him, oral and written. To his everlasting credit he never deigned to answer any of these attacks.

FAREWELL TO THE NATION

Far left: This anti-French cartoon reflects the tension that existed between France and the United States as a result of the French Revolution. In 1793, the French Government had dispatched to America a career diplomat, Genêt, to gain support for the French against the English. Genêt succeeded at first in arousing public opinion to the point of having 10,000 citizens stage a demonstration in Philadelphia against Washington, but he did not realize that this was just native American exuberance that did not mean a thing. Left: George Washington and his Cabinet. Above: "The Start of the Day" by J. L. Ferris. Washington is shown here with his wife and her two grandchildren who were their wards, saying grace before breakfast. In a letter to McHenry, then Secretary of War, Washington wrote: "I begin my diurnal course with the sun." After making the rounds of his property, "breakfast a little after seven o'clock . . . is ready." Then followed the rest of the daily occupations until the dinner hour. He ended his letter by saying that this description of his life for a day could be applied to an entire year.

There was nothing stated in the Constitution about the number of terms which a President could serve. It was assumed in some quarters that Washington would remain President for life. Nothing could have been further from his mind. A violent insolence on the part of his political opponents had replaced the almost religious respect which had once been shown him. His critics found fault with everything he was doing or had ever done. In 1796 the House of Representatives refused to adjourn for half an hour, as it had been its custom in the past few years, to honor his birthday. His control of his Cabinet was slipping. His prestige continued to be high with the masses who were spectators of the political play, but not with those who acted in it.

As his second term drew to a close, Washington had already decided not to serve a third time, a precedent which was unbroken until Franklin D. Roosevelt's time and which was reestablished, in writing, by the twenty-second amendment. On September 19, 1796, he communicated his decision to the public in a farewell address that was more a political testament than a formal leave-taking. Its advice and injunctions have had a deeper influence on American history than he could have anticipated. There has been considerable controversy over the question of authorship of the address. It seems reasonably well-established that though Hamilton, Madison and Jay all contributed suggestions, the basic ideas were Washington's.

In effect, his message, directed at the people of his day—a people unversed in political tactics "set free upon the great theatre of action" and possessed at last of a strong government—was to preserve, at all costs, the union which made the strength of that government. The people must not allow regional differences to weaken that union nor must a spirit of partisanship be allowed to prevail. In particular he warned against foreign entanglements: "The great rule of conduct for us in regard to foreign nations is, in extending our commercial relations to have with them as little *political* connection as possible. So far as we have already formed engagements let them be fulfilled with perfect good faith. Here let us stop. Europe has a set of primary interests which to us have none or a very remote relation. Hence she must be engaged in frequent controversies, the causes of which are essentially foreign to our concerns. . . ."

Few people were able to read it without remembering his military feats and his deep and abiding patriotism. They realized he was saying farewell to them forever. The esteem in which he had long been held came back almost immediately after he was out of office, and on his return journey to Mount Vernon in March, 1797, he was escorted through every town by groups of its leading citizens. This must have done something to obliterate the bitter memory of the vilifications that had been heaped upon him during his second term of office.

Below: Painting by
Edward Savage showing
Washington reviewing the western
army of the Continental forces
at Fort Cumberland in
Maryland on October 18, 1794.
This took place at the time
of the "Whiskey Rebellion."
Later Washington was called
back from private life to
resume command of the armed

forces in an extremely difficult
period for America.
Bottom of page:
Cartoon of a debate in
the Congress which appeared
shortly after Washington became
President. The behavior
of some of the representatives
was apparently not much
admired by some sections of
American public opinion.

FOREIGN RELATIONS

Washington's advice about foreign entanglements must have been inspired by the difficulties the young, new United States Government was experiencing with France. By the terms of our treaty of alliance with her we were committed to defend the French West Indian islands in the event of France being attacked by a European power; we agreed to allow French privateers to use our ports in time of war to outfit vessels and to bring in prizes; France alone could be granted this privilege, no other nation. Our commissioners in Paris, aware of the struggling states' need for money, signed without quibbling.

Then came the French Revolution which was exceedingly popular with the American masses but not with the Federalists whose disapproval deepened as the guillotine went to work. Very soon the French and English were at war again. France immediately opened up her West Indies' ports to American trade, and hundreds of American ships went into the business of transporting cargo between France and her possessions. The French, in accordance with the treaty of friendship and alliance, called upon us to come to their aid.

Americans in responsible positions viewed the situation with alarm. They knew we were in no position to help anyone. Our ports had been opened to French privateers who were bringing in captured British ships; the British naturally protested. The Administration was in a quandary. Should we ignore our great debt to France? But if we did not, we would surely not survive as a nation. The British, meantime, knowing the terms of the Franco-American treaty, had assumed we would honor it and had lost no time in instructing their cruisers and privateers to seize American ships bound for French ports. Washington's proclamation of neutrality so annoyed the French that they started seizing our ships.

The crisis eventually cooled down, but it left the Administration tingling. The terms of Jay's Treaty of 1794 with Great Britain did nothing to dispel Washington's wariness about foreign entanglements.

Two paintings by J. L. Ferris of Washington's family life. Above, with his wards, and below at the Mount Vernon school. The two children of Martha Custis Washington's first marriage lived with her at Mount Vernon. Both of them, who were very dear to Washington, died at a relatively early age. At the death of the boy, Jack, Washington adopted his two children, Eleanor Parke (Nelly) Custis and George Washington Custis. The latter was a cheerful ne'er-do-well, happy to bask in the reflected glory of his guardian. Nelly, beautiful and intelligent, was the President's pride and joy. She later married his favorite nephew, Lawrence Lewis.

*Below: Washington's funeral procession as
shown in a print by William Birch. This was held
in High Street, in Philadelphia, and was only
a mock funeral, for the actual burial took place in
Mount Vernon in the family plot. In 1802 his
wife Martha took her place beside him. People had
come to value her modesty and good sense.
"Unexpectedly placed in a prominent place," wrote a
contemporary of hers, "she behaved so well that she gave
rise to neither criticism nor envy." Right:
Contemporary print showing the death of Washington.*

LAST DAYS

George Washington's successor as President was John Adams, the Federalist candidate who received 71 votes. Jefferson, his opponent, had received 68 so he became Vice President. During Adams's term of office there was another crisis in the relations between the United States and France and war seemed imminent. Washington, who had retired to Mount Vernon in 1797 after having handed over the reins of government to his successor, was once more called upon. On Independence Day of 1798 he was offered the supreme command of the troops. He accepted but imposed very precise conditions, among them the right to appoint three major generals. However, the crisis passed; there was no war and Washington never again came out of retirement.

On December 12, 1799, he had gone horseback riding on his usual rounds. He caught a cold which developed into acute laryngitis. During the evening of December 14 it quickly degenerated into a pleurisy which gradually suffocated him. The contemporary treatment for most ailments, bleeding, had weakened him so much that two days later he was driven to say: "I feel myself going—you had better not take any more trouble about me; but let me go off quietly; I cannot last long." And later, as night was falling, he said to Dr. Craik who was attending him, "Doctor, I die hard, but I am not afraid to go." A few moments later he died.

His funeral was a simple affair, attended by neighbors. There were no heads of state, only friends and the mayor and council of Alexandria. A parting salute was fired by artillerists from Alexandria, and a body of local volunteers composed his military escort. His old friend Bryan Fairfax led the mourners behind the coffin which was followed by the General's riderless horse with his saddle, holsters and pistols.

The hero of an era had departed, but the record of his life remained.

Below: The Washington family vault at Mount Vernon. Over the doorway of the outer vault is the inscription: "Within this enclosure rest the remains of Gen. George Washington." Inside are two plain sarcophagi. On one are the coat of arms of the United States and the word "Washington"; on the other "Martha, Consort of Washington."

Washington and Napoleon have often been compared, but it is difficult to see any real points of comparison except that they were both generals and both commanded ragged armies—although Napoleon's armies did not long remain so.

Washington's greatness was a composite of simple virtues: honesty, courage, physical and spiritual, and tremendous force of character. Add to this great dignity and a sense of moderation and there is the moral picture of a great man. His moderation was often criticized, yet it was a golden virtue.

Despite his having been born into the upper strata of society he was a self-made man; everything he acquired, he earned through his own efforts and perseverance.

His life melts into the background of the times in which he lived. In fact, he was such an integral part of this background that at times his personality completely vanishes in the vast panorama of events. Yet, his example has been an inspiration to people of many nations and circumstances; for this was truly one of the great men of all time.

1732—February 22: His birth at Bridges Creek in Westmoreland County, Virginia.

1749—Appointed surveyor of Culpepper County, his first public employment.

1753—November: Expedition to Fort Leboeuf, held by the French, to find out their intentions.

1754—Appointed lieutenant-colonel and sent by the Ohio Company to their fort. May 28: Clash with a French detachment and death of nine French soldiers and one officer. October: Resigns from the army.

1755—February: Expeditionary force under General Braddock sent by the English. July 9: The French defeat the British at Monongahela and Braddock is killed. Washington is appointed Colonel and asked to reorganize the Virginia militia.

1758—November 25: The English Colonists defeat the French at Fort Duquesne.

1759—January 6: Marriage of George Washington with Martha Dandridge Custis.

1764—The passage of the Sugar Act arouses the first manifestations of dissidence.

1770—Boston Massacre.

1773—December 16: Boston Tea Party.

1774—First Continental Congress in Philadelphia. Washington attends as a delegate from Virginia.

1775—March: Patrick Henry's fiery speech in the House of Burgesses. April 19: Battle of Lexington and Concord. May: Second Continental Congress in Philadelphia. May 10: Capture by the Colonists of Fort Ticonderoga. Washington appointed Commander-in-Chief. June 17: Battle of Bunker Hill. July: Beginning of the siege of Boston.

1776—March: The English and Loyalists evacuate Boston. April-May: The Colonists lose the battle for Canada. July 4: Declaration of Independence. August: Washington defeated by Howe at the Battle of Long Island. September; the British occupy New York. November-December: The Americans pull back across New Jersey. December: Washington wins the Battle of Trenton.

1777—January 2: Washington wins the Battle of Princeton. June: Congress adopts the Stars and Stripes. July; Washington tries unsuccessfully, at the Battle of Brandywine, to keep Howe from entering Philadelphia. October 4: Defeat at Germantown. October 17: Burgoyne surrenders at Saratoga. December: France recognizes the U.S.A. Winter at Valley Forge.

1778—February 6: Treaty of Alliance with France signed. June 28: Battle of Monmouth. July: Wyoming Massacre. December: British capture Savannah.

1779—Abortive attempt by the Franco-American forces to recapture Savannah.

1780—May 12: Clinton's forces capture Charleston. August 16: American defeat at Camden.

1781—September 29: The Franco-American forces arrive in Yorktown and lay siege to the English. October 19: British surrender.

1782—November 30: Provisional agreement between the British and the Americans; American independence is recognized.

1783—September 3: Signing of the Peace Treaty at Versailles. December 23: Washington submits his resignation and retires to Mount Vernon.

1787—May: The Federal Constitutional Convention in Philadelphia unanimously elects Washington to preside over its deliberations.

1788—Nine of the States' legislatures ratify the Constitution.

1789—March 4: The Constitution comes into force. Washington is unanimously elected President of the United States. April 30: His inauguration.

1789-1797—Washington's two terms of office.

1796—Farewell Address.

1798—Called back from retirement to head an army in anticipation of war with France.

1799—December 14: Dies at Mount Vernon.